NATIONAL GEOGRAPH

D0100642

The Shopping List

Sue Whiting

Tony helps his dad at
the supermarket.
Tony gets a shopping basket
for all the things they need.

The shopping list shows what Tony and his dad need to buy.

Where are the bananas?

stone fruit

The bananas are with the fruits and vegetables.

Where are the sausages?

LATINA
3.66
5.25
5.25
4.41
SPECIAL PRICE
Food / way
6.99

The sausages are with the meat.

Where are the buns?

Butterbrook
Country Split
NOBLE RISE
SANDWICH WHITE BREAD
fabulous

The buns are with the bread.

Where is the ice cream?

AUSTRALIAN OWNED
BLUE RIBBON
BLUE RIBBON
CARAMELLO
TOP DECK
REAL DAIRY ICE CREAM
Paddle
20 WATER ICES

The ice cream is with the frozen foods.

Where are the toothbrushes?

Medium
Children
Hard
WHITE
TOILET
SOAP

The toothbrushes are with the toothpaste and soaps.

Where are the dog biscuits?

Multi
Biscrok
Multi
Biscrok
Biscrok

The dog biscuits are with the pet food.

Do Tony and his dad have everything on the list?

Yes, Tony and his dad have everything on the list!

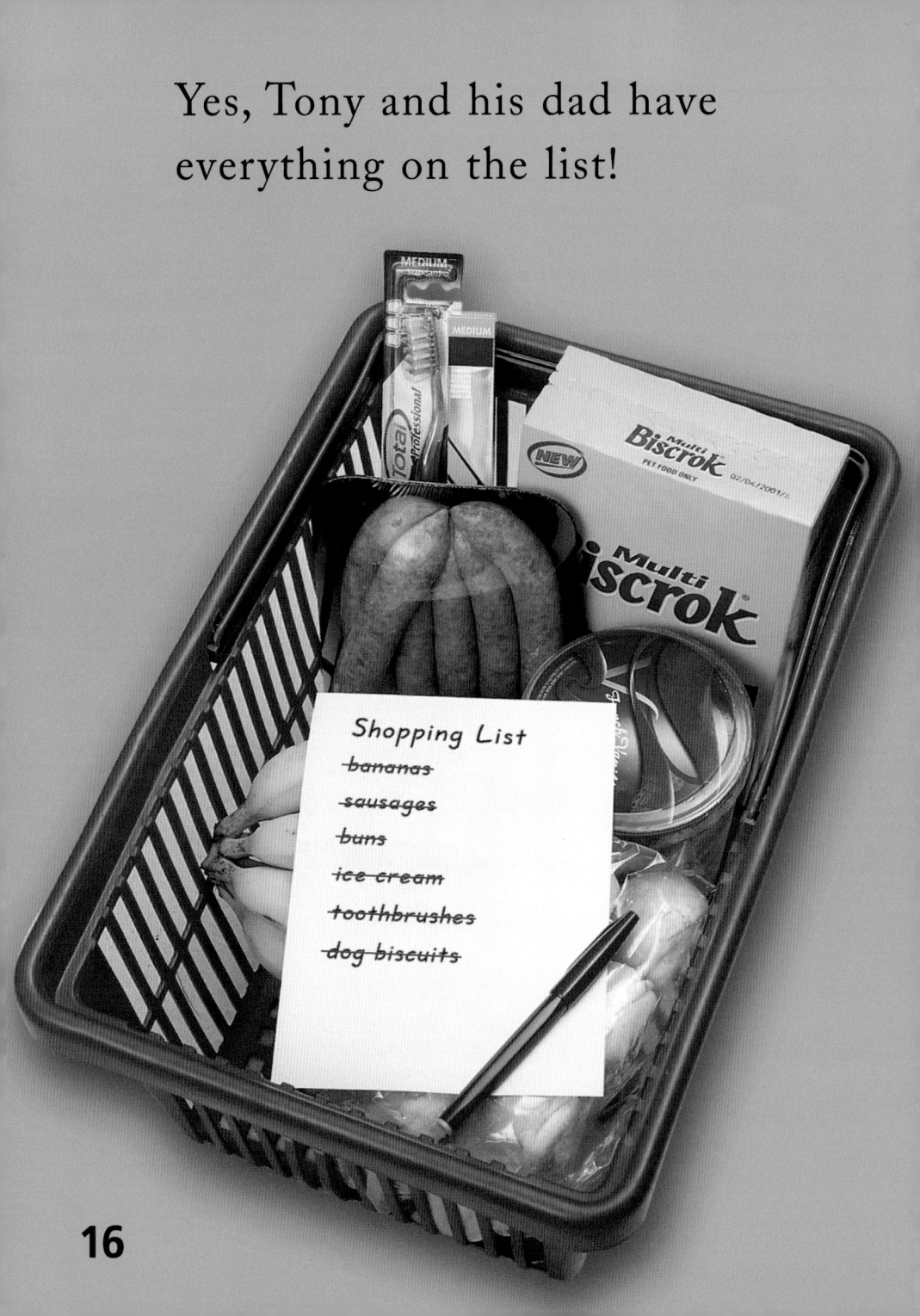